Librarianship in the Developing Countries

Librarianship
in the
Developing
Countries

LESTER ASHEIM

UNIVERSITY OF ILLINOIS PRESS
Urbana · Chicago · London
1966

Foreword

Since their inauguration in 1949, the Windsor Lectures in Librarianship have become one of the most distinguished series in the country dealing with books and related topics. The lecturer for 1966 was the twenty-first to participate in the Illinois programs.

Phineas Lawrence Windsor, in whose honor the lectureship was named, died in September 1965 at the ripe age of 94. His contributions to librarianship, during a career of more than forty years, were outstanding. From 1909 to 1940 he served as director of the Library and Library School of the University of Illinois. Under Professor Windsor's guidance the Library School became internationally known as a leading center for professional education, and the Library gained a position in the forefront of American university libraries. The endowed lectureship, created by several thousand alumni at the time of Professor Windsor's retirement, is both in recognition of his long-time leadership in the library world and fitting testimony of their loyalty, affection, and high esteem for him.

The Windsor Lecturer for 1966 is pre-eminently qualified to develop the theme of his three lectures, "Librarianship in the developing countries." From 1962 to 1966 he served as director of the American Library Association's International Relations Office. In that capacity he traveled widely abroad.

Mr. Asheim is a native of Spokane, Washington, and an alumnus of the University of Washington. During World War II he served in Alaska as a communications specialist in Signal Intelligence. Subsequently he entered the University of Chicago Graduate Library School, received a doctoral degree, and later served as dean of the school until joining the ALA staff.

The ALA International Relations Office, which Mr. Asheim headed, is a source of independent and unofficial advice for foundations, government agencies, and other

groups concerned with assistance to foreign libraries.
Viewing his position retrospectively, Mr. Asheim stated,
"The possibility of studying and exploring through foreign travel and of observing the state of library development all over the world, of coming in contact with
different cultures, I knew would be a chastening and
broadening experience." This is the rich background of
experience which the author brings to the present work.

15 September 1966   Robert B. Downs
                             Dean of Library Administration
                             University of Illinois

Contents

I

Some
Parallels and
Contrasts   1

II

Some
Overarching
Problems   33

III

The Role of
American
Librarianship   62

never vicariously — and certainly one of these is the phenomenon known as Culture Shock. It is a sensation experienced by almost everyone who is exposed to a way of life basically different from his own. It can be described, analyzed, and explained. But unless one experiences it directly, he does not know it, he only knows *about* it. And that is something quite different.

Culture Shock is not, as some people believe, limited to the kind of horror or dismay that one feels when a foreign situation is offensive or disgusting. It includes this, but it is far broader. It is brought about by any real clash of mores or values, and one is sometimes as deeply affected by the inconsequential as he is by the cosmic. Whenever the system of logic which we believe to be universal is suddenly challenged by a logical system to which we do not yet possess the key, we are likely to suffer Culture Shock. And if you are privileged, as I have been, to travel outside the insulated, cotton-lined grooves prepared for the first-class tourist, it can happen a dozen times a day, and every day of the year.

It is not my job here to document the exotic, strange, and bizarre corners of the globe (if you will pardon that contradiction in terms) that I have been fortunate enough to see during the past five years. My assignment, then and now, has been to deal with problems of librarianship. But there can be clashes of cultures even within the hoped-for One World of Librarianship too, and since there is something dramatic and enlightening about contrast and conflict, I should like to identify some the sense of an open collection of general materials designed for use by anyone who seeks information, recreation, self-education, or esthetic pleasure. There are so-called public libraries in some places, meaning that admission is not denied to anyone who wishes to enter, but they seldom attempt to collect and to organize their materials to meet the needs or the interests of what we loosely call "the average man." By our standards, these libraries would be seen either as public study rooms, primarily for students using their own books, or as special libraries for scholars browsing through the rare books, old books, and manuscripts that — in our country — would seldom find their way into public libraries at all.

Next our North American visitor would probably remark the almost total absence of service to children, in either the public libraries or the schools. That there are few school libraries might not surprise him too much; we are still far behind in the provision of the needed school libraries in our own country. But whereas children's books account for 50 per cent or more of the circulation in the average North American public library, most of the public libraries that do exist in other countries are essentially adult institutions. Children's services, if they occur at all, are likely to be housed and administered separately, specifically for children, and mainly as study areas rather than as general libraries. There is seldom any attempt to make the children's library an attractive foyer which will lead eventually to the adult collection; by and large, the children's materials consist of unselected accumulations of the local equivalent of comic books arranged in no order, subject to no selection process, and not available for loan. The love of books, the wonder of discovery, the opening of doors are not normally part of the child's experience in those few library situations that are provided for him.

In almost every country, our traveler will find at least one so-called national library, but again this name is given to the institution without the connotations we normally attach to it. A national union catalog, a national bibliography, a center of professional assistance to other libraries, or even a depository of the national publications is seldom to be found here. Very frequently the national library must, by default, serve a public library function, and as a result it is neither an adequate national library nor an adequate public library. It usually does have some valuable collections of manuscripts and rare books, but these have usually been acquired *en bloc* as gifts or memorials and remain, little used and seldom even cataloged, as isolated entities in the library, only remotely a part of the national treasure, and not even remotely a logical part of a popular library's service.

Generally speaking, the university libraries are likely to come closer to our own concept of a university library, but there are still some shocks. The so-called central library turns out not to be central at all; it contains no central catalog of the university's library holdings; it performs no centralized processing or acquisitions services; it does not circulate books; it may not even be open to undergraduates. Nor is it *the* library of the university; it is usually one of several faculty, departmental, and institute libraries, many of which are located in widely separated parts of the city. For example, in the University of Chile there are ninety-one separate libraries in different parts of Santiago and thirteen more in Valparaiso — with no single catalog that lists in any one place the materials available in this multitude of outlets. Within a single faculty — philosophy and education — there are thirty-eight libraries, some of which are under lock and key, and among those who are not permitted access to them is the head librarian of the faculty.

Each of these separate libraries in a university may have its own rules and regulations, its own systems — or no system at all — of cataloging and classification, its own restrictions on use, and complete independence of any centralized administrative oversight. There is seldom cooperation among them for exchange of information, interlibrary loan, or coordinated acquisition. The role of the central library is often merely that of a dumping ground for those books which none of the other libraries wants, and it is therefore frequently the least-used by students of any of the university's libraries.

When, finally, our traveling librarian comes to the special libraries (and here we must include some of the stronger faculty libraries), he may suddenly find the kind of libraries with which he is more familiar. This in itself is almost as great a shock as the deprivation he has been discovering elsewhere. In a country where there seems to be little organized information and small demand for it, suddenly he finds advanced systems of information retrieval; in a country where even the simplest of card catalogs is seldom provided, he finds centers of documentation at an advanced stage of development; in a country where the "librarian" of most institutions has had no professional training and exhibits no interest in the field, he finds Ph.D.'s from the leading graduate library schools of Europe and the United States. It is difficult to know whether to be delighted or disturbed; are these libraries and information centers really serving a purpose, or are they merely an empty symbol, necessary to the desired national image, which must have a twentieth-century surface despite the seventeenth-century reality behind it? At best, one notes that it is only in the areas of science and technology that these evidences of progress are to be seen; the traditional libraries remain as they were three hundred years ago. Does this mean that the humanities and the social sciences still do not require that their professors and scholars have access to information? In these countries is it only the medical doctor or the atomic scientist who must know his business in order to succeed in his field?

One raises this snobbish and cynical question partly because of the culture shocks he has already encountered. The familiar cues by which he orders his experience in his own environment have failed him so often in an alien land that he begins to suspect them all. He no longer takes at face value the handsome buildings, the shiny new machines, the polished jargon of explanation and justification that his tour guide reels off to describe the alleged state of the art. He has seen too many research collections from which no research has ever come, too many handsome marble fronts on buildings never completed inside, too many book collections to which access is forbidden, too many catalogs that do not provide a key to the collection they are supposed to index, too many machines that have not yet been put into use for want of a trained operator or a simple spare part, too many reference sets in mint condition, too many serial runs broken off somewhere in the middle when foreign aid ran out.

Since, obviously, this account is essentially autobiographical, and the unidentified North American librarian who acts as my protagonist in this account is obviously I, let me cite some specific instances that led me to such a jaundiced summary. I have tried very hard not to use an isolated instance as a norm; wherever I refer to a specific, let me assure you that it is merely a representative of many, many such along the route in the past five years — and that it is not an aberration of a single country. These have been repeated and repeated, in country after country, in both hemispheres, and on four of the seven continents. They are, indeed, examples which would no longer produce in me the Culture Shock that I once experienced. They now represent not surprise but expectation — and the real surprises are those instances where one finds the kind of library, librarian, and library service that he carries in his mind as a standard. Let me repeat, there are such examples in many of the places I have visited and I apologize to the good ones for dwelling on the less good. But it is the less good that need to be helped, and it was to offer help that I undertook my travels. It is one of the hazards of any profession that its practitioners concentrate on the worst rather than on the best that comes before them. The doctor must, after all, treat the sick, not the well.

Let us start with the problem of access. It is a first observation of any visiting librarian in any type of library in the developing countries that the books are generally in locked cases and closed stacks. It is not unusual to find bookshelves fifteen to eighteen feet high, where the books cannot be reached or even identified. Browsing along the shelves and the surprise benefits of serendipity are denied the users of libraries. This is an unfortunate barrier, but there are ways to surmount it, of course. The most familiar of these are a catalog and a system of classification, and another early observation is that librarians in the underdeveloped countries, both trained and untrained, are devoted to cataloging and classification. "Fair enough," you think, but it is at this point that our standard cues fail us and the assumptions that we normally make let us down. We cannot assume that because a book bears a classification number, that number will be used for any of the standard reasons we have for classifying books. Nor can we assume that because a card catalog exists, it is therefore a tool for identifying the library's holdings and locating them. I have learned not to stop with the verification that there is a card catalog. It is always well, I have discovered, to look at it, and to try to find in it an entry for a book or two that I have seen on the shelves.

Are the cards arranged alphabetically by author? Not necessarily, and certainly not in many Asian countries. Alphabetically by title? Alphabetically at all? By some system of subject approach? It is often very difficult to tell by looking at the drawer labels, or even within the drawers, and the staff person in charge, even though he be the director of the library, is often not able to tell you. But if he is trained, or at least sophisticated, it is likely that the arrangement will be designated as a classified catalog, and that the call numbers are used as the basis of the arrangement. But that is all that the classification number is used for, although it is carefully and usually unnecessarily carried out to five decimal places. Shelving, after all that detailed exercise in classification, is frequently by fixed location in accession order, or by size. As for that classified catalog, it turns out, more often than not, to be merely a kind of shelf list, with one card per title by its single classification number, and with no index whatsoever to the significance of the numbers.

How then does the patron find the book he wants through the catalog? You will not believe how frequently I have raised this question with the persons in charge of the library only to be met with complete lack of comprehension. Apparently this question has never occurred to them; if a patron wants a book on international relations of Transjordan with the United States, he must know in advance that the number is 327.5695073. That this is highly unlikely does not much bother the librarian because it is even more unlikely that a library user will come with that kind of question in the first place. The library's patron is typically a user of the premises, but not of the books.

This, of course, reflects the teaching method which prevails in most parts of the world outside the United States, since teaching method affects not only curricular use of books, but lifelong attitudes toward book use. In a report on the Turkish book industry, this description occurs:

Teaching methods are antiquated. Teachers require that their students memorize the textbooks. The . . . book . . . is something to memorize, not necessarily to understand, and never to question. . . . Teachers seldom suggest titles to be read in conjunction with their courses. They are usually unaware of such materials themselves. Reading of material outside textbooks is frowned upon by most parents and Ministry of Education inspectors. The tendency of the Ministry is to "prevent the entry of subversive material into the schools" rather than to encourage the reading of books.[1]

This particular passage refers to Turkey, but it would apply equally well to the rest of the Middle East, Latin

[1] Mehmet Deger Durukan, "A Report on the Turkish Book Industry" (February, 1965, Franklin Book Programs Book Industry Seminar), New York, 1965, p. 5.

America, and most of Asia and Africa. Under these circumstances it is not so surprising that most reading rooms in libraries of all kinds are empty of books. Chairs and tables are the only requirements; the students will supply their own textbooks and the mimeographed copies of the lecture notes which will meet all of their reading needs.

But even this use of libraries is made difficult. To those of us who have been trying to make our libraries attractive and inviting, the simple business of admission to the library's facilities seems terribly forbidding. It is not typical, for example, that any student may walk into the university library by the front door. The handsome entrance to the building, through which the visiting dignitary is ushered, is not necessarily the means of access to the building for the student. He must go through some other narrow control point where he surrenders his identification card, deposits his briefcase, checks his coat, and establishes his possession of clean hands and a pure heart. Underclassmen are frequently not allowed to enter the faculty and departmental libraries at all, nor to borrow books from even the central library. Book use is not only discouraged by teaching method, it is virtually prohibited by the rules to underclassmen. Even for upperclassmen and graduate students, use of the faculty libraries is usually restricted to the students of the particular discipline. This causes much less distress than you might think, since no catalog of the departmental library's holdings is available outside it own walls and so even a research student is unlikely to be led to seek a title outside his own faculty collection.

With so many restrictions on the use of what little space is available, the public and national libraries are much in demand by the students as study rooms and are almost always filled to capacity. The would-be user of any library may have to wait for hours for a seat to become vacant; he is permitted to enter only if he has a seat assignment. But what if a student or nonstudent adult patron merely wishes to be allowed to enter the building to check the card catalog, charge out a book, and depart? Since there is so seldom a card catalog that the patron can use, and since books do not circulate, this is a naive question. What is more, it has not yet occurred, in most cases, to any librarian, student, instructor, or reader to raise it.

There are, as additional barriers to pleasurable library use, elaborate precautionary systems to guard against the removal of books, not only from the building, but even from the shelves. An ingenious device, of which many variants may be found in other libraries and in other countries, is one that I observed in Latin America. Upon entrance each patron is given a square metal tag, which he must surrender upon leaving. If he applies for a book to use while in the library, the square tag is exchanged by the desk attendant for a triangular one. When the book is returned, the tags are exchanged again. Thus no one can leave the building or retrieve his personal belongings and his all-important identification card if he is still carrying a triangular tag. It is an extremely simple but effective system for insuring against book loss and, to a very large extent, against book use as well.

In another library I visited, although the shelves are open in the reading rooms, a patron may not approach them even to browse; an attendant is the only one who is permitted to touch a book on the shelf. In many other libraries, it is quite literally true that the books are behind chicken wire, or at least glass-fronted, locked cabinets, and the patron must try to peer through to find a title that seems to be of interest to him, then point it out to the attendant who will hand it to him for use within the building. And admission may require not merely the identification card of the student, but a registration procedure involving verified references and recommendations from those highly placed, which can bar admission to many a reader whose seriousness seems insufficiently documented to the head librarian. In such situations it is discouraging to note how frequently the necessary documentation reflects class and caste distinctions, as does, of course, the registration fee which still continues to be exacted in some places.

It is true that the registration fee is gradually disappearing, but a system of cash deposit for the borrowing of books still prevails in many places, even in universities where the student has already been assessed a library fee. One of the most elaborate of these requires that the patron must, for each individual book borrowed, leave a deposit equal to the price of the book. This is not a standing deposit against borrowing in general, but a book-by-book transaction, with the entire sum returned to the patron each time he brings back his book. A whole new deposit procedure must be instituted for the next loan. A major part of the task of adding any book to this collection then, even if it be a donation, is the search for a record of its price, since, if the price is not marked in the book, it is not permitted to circulate because the attendant cannot know how much deposit to charge. Imagine the amount of record-keeping involved to account for a sum that would not pay for the cost of replacing the book anyway!

What strikes one here, as it did in so many of my exchanges with librarians over the use and purpose of the card catalog or the classification scheme, is the commitment to procedures and routines nonconducive to the ends for which they were established. Somewhere along the line someone determined that there shall be a deposit charged for each book borrowed, or that a card catalog must be set up, or that every catalog card must have a call number in an upper corner. It may even have made sense at the time. So the first of the sheep leaped over the fence, and all of the sheep that follow continue the high leap, although the top rung has long since fallen down and it would now be possible simply to walk through. The disturbing thought is that so often that first decision may have been made by an American or other foreign expert, brought in to introduce method and system, who merely introduced a practice he was used to at home. One is forced to speculate whether the question "Why?" was ever asked, even at the beginning.

There is another aspect of access which strikes the foreign visitor — the complete absence of what we know as reference service. In very few libraries of any type is there a reference department or a reference librarian designated to give the patron bibliographical and other assistance in finding information within the books and other materials of the collection. Here again we run into some semantic problems: I have often asked if reference service is given, and I am usually assured that it is. But it turns out that reference service is seen merely as a kind of directional and paging assistance. If the patron knows the author and the title of the book he wants, the attendant can — often — find it for him. This is what is meant by reference service. It almost never means the searching down of wanted facts through a variety of sources, the bringing together a list of useful materials on a given subject, the analyzing of content so that a specific piece of information can be found within a larger work. Even the reference tools that do exist in some of the collections are merely *there;* the staff person does not offer assistance in their use, and in most cases is incapable of using them himself. Indeed, reference service as we know it is so little a part of the librarian's task that it is frequently not even included in the curricula of the training programs for librarians.

It should come as no surprise, therefore, that book

selection in our terms is also very infrequently encountered. In many of the developing countries, a great part of the collection depends upon gifts and exchanges, and anything that comes in is accepted. Where book budgets are available, they are usually quite limited, and in any case the selector is seldom the librarian. In the universities and schools, selection is completely in faculty hands, often with final authority resting with a committee of deans or even the vice-chancellor. Consequently what falls between departmental or personal interests may never find its way into the collection at all, unless random gifts happen to coincide with a need. The odds against that, as you can guess, are great indeed.

Whatever purchasing is done is done primarily through the local bookstore. In the best of instances, the storekeeper may send examples of his latest stock to the library for examination and selection; in the usual situation, the selector must check the bookstore shelves periodically in the hope of running down what he wants and getting it before private purchasers have picked over the stock; in the worst of situations, a blanket order is given to the lowest bidder who may substitute as much as 15 per cent of an order with any rejects and slow sellers he wants to unload. So even in the best of situations, the actual selection is made by the bookseller, whose objectives are seldom those of a serious librarian.

Such a system is bad enough as a means for running down the needed books; it is even worse for any kind of systematic control of journal acquisition. The difficult task of service and follow-up, complicated and time-consuming in the best of conditions, is virtually abandoned under these circumstances. While many of the libraries have a serial record — I nearly said "keep" a serial record but that implies far greater attention to currency than would be accurate — few ever try to follow through on missing issues or check on delays or gaps in delivery. Like the perfunctory card catalog, the Cardex file for serial records is a conventional accessory, but not a functional tool.

You may wonder why a professional librarian is needed if there is no responsibility in his hands for book selection, reference work, reader services, or administrative control. The same question has already been raised and answered in most of these countries: there is no need for a professional librarian, except to assign classification numbers and to create catalogs. Traditionally in the national libraries and the universities, the title of librarian is merely an honorary one, given to a man of letters, a historian, or an academic dean who continues to hold full-time responsibilities elsewhere and who pays little or no attention to the planning, organization, supervision, and control that are the task of a librarian in our society. Understandably one cannot expect professional concern about library management or library goals from that quarter.

This is not to say that there are no trained librarians. There are some, and some of them would be an asset to the profession in any country in the world. But all too frequently they are held subordinate to the non-librarians who hold the director's title, and their administrative responsibility is limited to personal accountability for any book loss. The low status of the librarian is clearly revealed in such a structure, and it is a status that cannot be altered readily, even if there were more well-trained librarians available to take the responsible positions. Let me cite an illustrative anecdote: in one Middle Eastern country, an eminent professor of archaeology who had done some advanced study in the United States was assigned, upon his return to his homeland, to take charge of the library of the faculty of letters, in addition to his full-time academic responsibilities. None of his protests of lack of interest and lack of training were of any avail; he had been to the States and had seen American libraries, hadn't he? Very well, he could easily do all that a librarian needs to do. When he produced his trump card — that he had married an American girl with a graduate degree from one of the leading American library schools — the reaction of the university administration was one of delight. Fine — all the more reason for him to take the appointment; he could ask his wife anything he needed to know. Never once did it occur to them that a professionally trained person should be put in charge; the post goes to an academic who may (but need not) use librarians for advice.

Where such an attitude prevails, it is to be expected that library needs carry a very low priority in the competition with other demands upon the limited budgets of the university, the city, or the national government. There is no question about where to put the available funds, as between a science laboratory or a library, a public administration professor or a librarian, a computer or a collection of books. Those in a position to make decisions on such matters have probably never seen a library from which they could derive any service or benefit; those in charge of the libraries are more interested in their own subject fields than in this secondary obligation that they did not seek; those with some library training and a knowledge of the library's potential are not in a position to present the case.

The low status of the librarian carries other hazards with it. Usually library salaries are so low that most librarians, and teachers of librarianship, must carry additional jobs to eke out their subsistence. That being so, there is seldom time for the planning, organization, and management that a professional librarian is supposed to give to his job. The persistence of so much that hampers the library services can be attributed to this — that the librarians just do not have the time or the support to work on changes. And since they do not, their professional contribution is limited, and the value of a trained person over an untrained person is difficult to establish. And thus we come the full round of the vicious circle.

Et cetera, et cetera. One could continue to ferret out horrible examples. It is easy to do, and it is not quite fair. It is the immediately discernible, surface phenomenon, flattering to the visitor who likes to compare the worst of another country with the best of his own. And after a while, the zest of the game palls; as one becomes more accustomed to the way things are he begins to see that there are as many parallels as there are contrasts, and that what horrifies him elsewhere is swallowed whole at home. The first step away from Culture Shock is a kind of counter-shock concerning our own practice, which we have not really ever examined as critically as we have been examining the practice abroad.

When we are forced to look at our own practice — and usually this occurs only when we return home from another part of the world and thus see for a while with the eyes of a visitor from another culture — we are likely to experience our Culture Shock in reverse. There is hardly a fault we have been deploring abroad of which we do not find instances on our own doorstep.

For example: we condemn the locked cases and the closed stacks that characterize the foreign library, yet closed stacks are a familiar phenomenon in the United States. I have never worked in a university library that did not have them. Locked cases, special permission collections, and other such barriers to free access are familiar to us, even in our public libraries. Sometimes we justify these restrictions on the grounds of limited space, on the difficulty of replacing the books, on the dangers of theft. All of these reasons prevail abroad, usually more urgently than here. As for the elaborate machinery to prevent book loss, I suggest that the square-tag system is more effective than our own experiments with magnetic plates and electronic alarms — and much less expensive.

Or take the example of the departmental library systems that prevail in the universities abroad. Once again I must admit that my own university library experience has exposed me to departmental libraries in great profusion on most North American campuses, and that it is not unheard of that different hours, different regulations on use, and even different classification systems might prevail among them. Nor is it unusual to find American universities with certain units spread out across the town, or in more than one city. We think nothing of it if a North American medical, dental, law, or business school is housed with its own library away from the central campus — and with rather strict departmental restrictions on the use of its collection. Somehow it only horrifies us in another country, not in our own. And it is chastening to have to answer, as I did, a librarian in Okinawa who wondered why American universities are so committed to the departmented fragmentation of the total collection (he cited Harvard) instead of recognizing the superior efficiency of a centralized collection like that of the University of the Ryukus. Up to that point I had been smugly self-satisfied in the conviction that all the world can plainly see that it is the American university library that demonstrates the sensible model of efficient centralization while the foreign university persists in the foolish and wasteful decentralized tradition. To see ourselves as others see us is one of the fringe benefits of foreign travel.

As for teaching method which relies on the lectures of the instructor and the single textbook rather than on wide reading, I merely refer you to the spate of critical writings about American education and your own experience. It is not unknown in the United States for a professor to reward those students whose examination papers contain a rote feedback of his own ideas; it is well known that many students can go pretty far along the academic route without, as our well-known expression has it, "cracking a book," and that our reserve book systems of which we are so proud serve to make it possible for an entire class to read exactly the textbook passages needed to pass the course without taking any chances on additional reading that might not pay off. There are, as a matter of fact, certain kinds of course content and subject areas where carefully chosen and directed reading may make more sense than wide and random reading, and some of our most highly thought-of experimental programs have featured the small list of prescribed texts which will be studied and re-studied intensively.

Nor need any school, college, or university librarian in this audience be reminded of the penchant of American faculty members to collect in their own offices the books they feel they want and need and to make them as inaccessible as possible except to a few special protégés to whom they dole out a recommended title as a special favor.

As for boards of education, parents, and others whose concern about school libraries rests on the desire "to prevent the entry of subversive material into the schools rather than to encourage the reading of books," this appears to be a far greater problem in the United States than in any other country, at least to our foreign students in American library schools, who are constantly amazed at the censorship, pressures, and interference with which American librarians have to contend. In no other country that I know of has it yet been deemed necessary to establish a special office and a special legal adviser within the library association to deal with nothing except these problems of interference with the wide provision of books.

The inadequacy of school libraries to deal with student needs and the overcrowding of public and scholarly libraries by students needing work space are problems of such urgent importance in the United States that we held a special "Conference Within a Conference" on the matter in 1963, and have been working on approaches to a solution ever since. The appointment of nonlibrarians to the post of director of the library, particularly in the academic world, can certainly happen here, as can the use of the trained librarian for routine tasks under the supervision of a scholar from some other discipline. The wider use of new devices, new approaches, and new concepts in the special libraries, as contrasted with the devotion in public and academic libraries to the traditional methods which frequently are no longer adequate to meet today's needs, is yet another phenomenon well known to librarians in the United States. This is, indeed, perhaps the most vociferously debated question in American librarianship at the moment, and to those who are urging the new and experimental methods, the situation must seem very like that in the countries we are pleased to call "underdeveloped." The impetus has come, here as there, not from the librarians but from scientists and technologists; presumably here too other fields can still survive without ready access to the latest information.

As for devotion to classification and cataloging, this too has been a favorite whipping boy within the profession in the United States, and the classic basis of the attack is that so many of our technical processes of all kinds seem to be based on a knowledge of how-to-do-it, but no analysis of why. Perhaps our card catalogs do not exhibit all of the faults that I enumerated in my account of catalogs abroad, but certainly we have many of the same *kinds* of faults if not to the same degree. It would not be difficult to cite many American examples of the kind of intransigent adherence to rules which subverts the very purpose that the rules are meant to serve. In fact, I myself once devoted an entire public address to just such a theme.[2]

Last, it is nothing new to American librarians to hear that the status of librarians is low compared to that in other vocations and professions, that other disciplines get first consideration for support and attention, and that there is a tremendous shortage of trained people to per-

[2] Lester Asheim, "Wake Up! It's Time for Your Sleeping Pill," *Library Journal,* 85 (January 15, 1960), 190-194.

form the necessary professional tasks. If there is one concept that is held universally by librarians, it is the conviction that we are the stepchild of the professions.

These parallels, although they describe problems of a similar kind, do not recognize sufficiently clearly the differences in degree. While it is true that one can find an example in the United States to match virtually every instance I have cited for the developing countries, there is a considerable difference between a practice which constitutes a small breakdown in the system, and a practice which is, essentially, the system itself. The locked case is a deviation from our norm, and in a sense in conflict with our basic policy of freedom of access. We see it as the exception rather than the rule, and we attempt in every way possible to counteract it through indirect approaches to the material. Thus, our card catalogs, in spite of the faults that we might find with them, are designed to serve as public keys to the collection, and many of the inconsistencies and conflicts that occur within them derive from our attempts to set them up to reflect the approach of the patron. Our classification schemes are pragmatic devices to help the user, not ideal philosophical systems to order the universe of knowledge. The locked case is normally designed to protect the book *for* the user, not from him, and all of our machinery of cataloging and classification is meant to put the book and the information it contains into the reader's hands, locked case or no. It is fair enough to say, I think, that we have the occasional locked case whereas the developing libraries abroad have the occasional open shelf. Such a difference is more important than the apparent similarity.

Again, looking at the highly departmentalized university library systems, I think we can say that ours represent a kind of compromise between the ideal of the librarian and the ideal of the specialized user, and in none of the United States universities which break up their holdings into subject collections will you find — I trust — an instance in which there is not somewhere, for public consultation, a central union catalog which lists every book owned by the university with an indication of its location. Indeed, this statement touches upon the key difference: in our thinking, the books are owned by the university and are housed in different locations to maximize their most effective use. In most foreign libraries, the books are owned by the faculties, and no other part of the university has any reason to assume a right to access. This regulation is so strong that a book no longer wanted by one department may not, in many instances, be transferred to another which could use it; the individual inventories are absolutely binding upon the location of the book and the use that can be made of it, and there are often strict regulations against even the loan of a book outside its parent department for any reason whatsoever.

When we speak of the inadequacy of school libraries in the United States, the standard on which we base our complaint is out of sight for the citizens of most other countries, and our mediocre looks better than their best. When we speak of the low status of librarians, the low priority given to library needs, and the inadequate salaries of librarians, we do so in a country where the federal government has, in the past ten years, authorized hundreds of millions of dollars for the improvement of library services through specific library legislation or special library titles in other major bills. To insist upon parallels under such circumstances is highly unrealistic. The differences in degree are so great that they actually become differences in kind. A country of close to 14 million people with only two or three trained librarians (this is an actual figure) is talking about a different kind of shortage than is the librarian of an institution which, in addition to its present professional staff of 250 people, could use an additional ten to make possible new services and more flexibility in vacation schedules. Instead of speaking of "Parallels and Contrasts," I suppose I should really underline the parallels *as* contrasts.

My purpose in emphasizing the differences is not to demonstrate that our system is better. "Better" and "less good" are terms which have meaning only if we specify better or less good *for what* — and that is precisely the point I am trying to make. Even when we use the same terminology we may not be referring to the same things, and the reason we do not mean the same things is that we may have an entirely different set of objectives and an entirely different scale of values, shaped by influences quite outside the field of librarianship itself. Despite the apparent similarities — we have buildings called libraries which house book collections — there is one very real difference in basic philosophy that alters the purposes for which we employ the librarian's tools, even when the tools are, or appear to be, essentially the same ones. That big, overriding difference seems to me to rest on the amount of emphasis we place upon the importance of *service to readers*. In most of the foreign libraries I have been including in my generalizations, the book is more important than its user. The system that has been devised is designed primarily to protect the book and preserve it; in some cases this is the entire end of librarianship. The opposite extreme is to make the reader more important than the book, and many North American librarians have expressed this tenet boldly: "I don't mind when a book is missing; it means someone is using it." The middle ground, which tries to make the book and the reader equally important, is capable of many gradations; the lengths to which we are willing to go to protect the book in order that it shall be available when a reader wants it define the degree to which we are moving toward one or the other extreme.

In the United States, we tend to feel a loyalty to the reader more than to the book. We open our shelves, knowing that some books will be stolen or mutilated. We offer reference service to all, knowing that we will wear out some of our expensive reference tools on questions of minor importance. We allow books to circulate, knowing that some will never be returned. We purchase books with more attention to their content than to their format or their value as artifacts. We see a need to give the reader what he wants, sometimes more than to buy the books that deserve representation on the shelves of a library, especially if they will have no current readers. Along this continuum, with the primacy of the reader on one end and the primacy of the book on the other, many librarians both from within the United States and outside it tend to move a bit toward the center. But by and large, we tip the seesaw on the reader's end, and they tip it toward the book. We cannot possibly meet in the middle without each of us giving up a great deal that we strongly believe in.

Nevertheless, I have introduced the concept of the parallel for two reasons. Even though we must immediately correct it — or rather, precisely because we must immediately correct it — it serves to illustrate an extremely important point. Although the problems seem to be the same because of our generalized terminology and because, in a rough way, they are similar in kind, we must guard very carefully against a corollary assumption that the solutions we have worked out for our problems can therefore be carried over to solve theirs. This is a point that will be examined later, and I merely note it here. But it may be the most important point I can make in these presentations, and it does no harm to refer to it more than once.

The other reason for introducing the concept of the parallel is also a pedagogical one. It is my belief that my condemnation of a locked bookcase in Asia or the Middle East is accepted by Americans with vigorous approval, whereas when I couple our own locked cases with those of other countries, a defensive reflex is immediately provoked: "There are reasons for ours"; "it is not quite so simple as all that"; "you overlook some important considerations"; etc. Quite true — but no less true abroad. There are reasons in Asia too, and the denigration of the other system also involves oversimplification and the omission of certain circumstances.

You may remember that I began with a reference to Culture Shock, which I said occurred whenever the system of logic in which we believe is challenged by a logical system to which we do not yet possess the key. It is not the other system that must be corrected, but the absence of the key. There are usually reasons for what people do, even if they are not our reasons. Before we condemn out of hand a pattern of behavior which happens not to fit our preconceptions, we should try to find out what the reasons were that led to it. We may still not accept the reasons as valid for us, but we may discover a different context of validity for evaluating the behavior pattern and its use by others.

One such context, it seems to me, is provided by the philosophy of library service that has emerged even in this short comparative analysis: the philosophy of primacy of the book over the reader. Before we denounce it, we should try to understand how it came into being. It obviously derives in part from the difference in economic circumstances and the comparative ability to pay, but it goes far behind and beyond that. It is my hope that Chapter II, by exploring some of the reasons that led to it, may help to dispel some of the strangeness which inhibits our understanding and appreciation of library practice in other countries.

when he travels in other cultures. Unfortunately, despite our intellectual recognition of this principle we still carry with us predispositions and habits of thought that convince us that certain values and certain goals must be universal. We can understand that books will be in Arabic in the Middle East and Spanish in Latin America, but we cannot believe that their readers will think differently than we about the virtues of open access, wide selection, freedom of choice, and, indeed, reading itself. That it is a purely local rather than universal principle that places these values high on our scale is something very hard for us to grasp.

I do not mean to say that we think that literacy is universal, that schooling is available to everyone, or that all societies necessarily place a high value on reading and writing or great reliance on print as a source of communication. After all, we have been exposed to anthropological studies of primitive societies; indeed, one of our difficulties is that we are likely to know more about growing up in New Guinea than we know about maturing in Montevideo. We are able to accept the contrasts between our society and another if all aspects of the environment are consistent; we do not expect a half-naked tribe in the jungle to form a Friends of the Public Library group. But when we are in a society that has schools, colleges, and universities, that publishes books and boasts bookstores, that builds libraries and trains librarians, we find it very difficult to accept the fact that it may nevertheless have an entirely different kind of expectation about its books, its schools, and its libraries. As I said earlier, though we use the same words, or even share the same tongue, it does not necessarily follow that we speak the same language.

There are many social and historical influences that shape the way a people feels about society and its institutions. Our romantic view of democracy, that derives from an accident of time (the late eighteenth century) and of place (the new and boundless world of the frontier), has led us to develop public libraries characterized by equality of access, maximum availability, and an emphasis on ease of use and broad popular appeal — to reflect our ideals about the democratic necessity of universal education. Given this bias, it is inevitable that we should, as was suggested in Chapter I, place the reader (i.e., a human being) above the book (i.e., a thing, however valuable, beautiful, or rare). But societies that have developed under different circumstances have taken a different view, one that evolves just as logically and rationally from its premises as our view has developed from ours. And these differences are not only apparent on the broad philosophical level but in every aspect of life and living.

Let me touch lightly on a few of these influences. I will not, for the time being, deal specifically with libraries but rather with the nature of the society. I assume that you will, as librarians, automatically supply for yourselves the library implications of these social forces. Take, for example, the effect of an aristocratic tradition. Where the established way of life accepts a ruling class, the ideal of universal education is unthinkable. Where one is born to his condition and inherits his power, no one without this predestined position can expect to change his status through individual effort. Even those who do not enjoy the advantages of the upper class are conditioned to accept this fact as inevitable; the ruled are usually as convinced as the rulers that there are special qualities of leadership which are inherent in the upper classes which lower classes cannot attain. Therefore it follows that equality of educational opportunity can serve no useful social purpose; to give education to everyone is merely a costly waste of time and effort which unfits the majority to perform the tasks suited to their station.

The kind of education that any nation offers supports its own beliefs and institutions, and formal education in a class-conscious society tends to confirm the belief of the educated that they possess particular natural qualifications which are absent in others. Such an education must, by definition, be limited to the elect; to open it to others is virtually to destroy its basic tenets. The educated classes in an aristocratic society are convinced that broader, wider, mass education must inevitably dilute its quality, and certainly they are right that the nature and content of education would be changed by throwing it open. In many of the developing nations an active campaign of informal indoctrination supports the closed formal system, urging each citizen to accept his particular given place and role in the building of the society. So the system that prevails is designed quite specifically to keep people out, not to let them in.

Inevitable in any society, including our own, is the selfish desire to preserve the special privilege which adheres to the class. Those who have it do not willingly relinquish it, and those who, in this generation of rising expectations, aspire to push up are much more motivated by the desire personally to enter this realm of privilege than, despite the oratory and the slogans, to abolish it. This conflict of philosophies is one of the great problems facing many of the developing countries. The increase in opportunities for higher education notwithstanding, it is still restricted to a very small proportion of the total population. On the basis of their numbers the members of this group still represent an elite. And the education they seek is an elite education designed to fit the educated for the role they would have played in the aristocratic society. Thus, higher education did not, and still does not, deal with practical subject matter, since the educated man was not expected to do the work which was seen as properly the task of the middle and lower classes. This was a perfectly suitable concept of education's role as long as the status quo was maintained, but it is not unusual, in today's changing world, to find that demands are being made upon the educated for skills they do not have or — equally likely — that they are unwilling to exercise. In the newer societies particularly it is being found over and over again that education, which was meant to provide society with men better equipped to deal with its problems, has turned out instead a self-appointed elect which refuses to sully its hands with the tasks that must be met.

Nor is this merely a problem at the top. It is not only the philosopher-king who today needs education; the ability to read and write, to run machines, to function in a complex urban community all require education too. Yet someone who is well enough educated to operate a typewriter is, in many countries, a member of so small and special a company that he would disdain to be a typist. And so the shortage of educated and trained people is felt at every level, and the big job cannot be accomplished because there is nobody capable or willing to do the smaller job upon which the big one depends. Thus all of society is deprived, not just those who are denied educational opportunity. But the educated are not yet able to see this because the system under which they were educated was not concerned with all of society but only that portion of it to which education once exclusively catered.

I have deliberately painted an extreme picture of the aristocratic tradition, of course, but many of today's societies, even those which call themselves democratic, have evolved from a system very like the one I have described, and have been influenced in their thinking and their values by such considerations. Certainly it is not difficult to find states in which equal rights and opportunities are deliberately withheld from certain classes in order to protect the privileges and the ascendancy of those now in authority. In any such situation, education is likely to be one of the rights most diligently restricted, for exactly the reasons that the ideal democratic society would wish to make education available to all.

Another important tradition that continues to exert a great influence over the thinking and the action of many countries is that of deference to age, authority, and the past. This has provided a stability and a standard that has preserved many of these nations, but it also has imposed a curb on independent thought and investigation. Where authority — parental, religious, political — must be accepted without question, there is little opportunity for innovation and experimentation, for critical exploration and objective analysis.

Most particularly in such a tradition, there is little opportunity for the young to make a contribution while they still have new ideas and the drive to push them forword. By the time a man has gained the years and experience to which a tradition-oriented society will listen, he has been absorbed into the tradition himself. Change is not impossible, but it must inevitably come very slowly — too slowly these days for many of the best of the younger generation who have the most to offer. The brain drain is a problem for every country which represents a comparatively closed society; the lure is much less the offer of more money than it is the opportunity for self-fulfillment.

There is another characteristic of a society of this kind. Primary loyalty is given to the family, the clan, the tribe, rather than to the nation as a whole. Again this makes for a kind of stability and a kind of strength that must be admired. On the other hand, it often leads to a narrowness of vision that denies loyalty or duty to any outside the defined ring. Where there is no obligation to the wider society, any kind of cooperative effort on a broader scale is almost impossible to initiate. The positive values of tribal loyalty have their negative and dark side in a suspicion, distrust, and hatred of all outsiders — not just of strangers and foreigners, but even of those of one's own country, city, or neighborhood if they are not within the clique. And it leads to the kind of familial obligation which in our society borders on the reprehensible, the favoritism which we define as "corruption" in many of our institutions. Perhaps no more graphic example can be found of the nature of Culture Shock than our automatic revulsion against the nepotism practiced by anyone in authority in certain societies, and their equally violent reaction against our habit of separating ourselves from our parents, grandparents, and other family members. Each side looks with distaste on the other's practices, and both are firmly convinced that "all reason is against it" — as indeed it is, given the basic premise upon which each side builds its social ethic.

The outstanding tendencies of both the aristocratic tradition and the tradition of higher authority are intensified, of course, by colonialism. It can easily be seen that deference to authority is an important ingredient of colonial control. Coupled with it, one usually finds also the arrogation of special privileges for the governing class. Now it must be remembered that most of the new nations, and a great many of the older but underdeveloped ones, were under colonial control until only very recently. Colonial languages, literature, government, and social influences dominated and still have their effect. These standards, all too frequently, sustain and support existing predispositions in the culture, and continue to exert a strong influence long after they have been officially abolished.

There were, in addition, some special variations on these themes that served to deepen their effect. In many cases, the most authoritative positions in the colonial civil service and in commerce were reserved for the foreigners, and as a result, even fewer opportunities were available to the nationals to use their skills and qualifications. Thus, in addition to the stringent limitations placed upon their chances for formal education, there were even more limited opportunities for them to get training in leadership through direct experience. Even more than under their own systems, their only chance ever to make much of themselves lay outside their own countries. The inevitable frustration has led the intellectuals into the political arena and accounts for the violence of their reaction when the time finally came to move from under the colonial controls.

Where a civil service which would absorb the local citizens did exist, it was, naturally enough, set up to maximize control. Routines and procedures were devised to keep to a minimum the amount of decision-making that would be required of the civil servant. The entire organization was planned to discourage variations, adaptations, or innovation. The good old-fashioned red tape, from which our derisive phrase comes, is still in use in most of the former British colonies because this is the system and the type of organization which was taken to be the model of progressive administrative expertise and has now come to represent efficient administration in many of the newly independent nations whose leaders have carried over the procedures for which they were trained and to which they have become accustomed. Extremely effective for maintaining the status quo, the system is almost completely wrong for fostering progress and nourishing independence. It has left the new nations with nineteenth-century tools with which to do a twentieth-century job.

It should not be inferred that these deterrents to progress were always deliberately devised for that purpose. The representatives of foreign nations who first came to settle and to rule in Africa, Asia, and elsewhere often brought with them the best that they remembered from their own countries. The French and British university systems, for example, carefully transplanted overseas, represented a high standard of achievement toward which many of the native populations could never have aspired on their own. But the expatriates themselves were held back by their distance from home and from communication with later developments. Nostalgia for the "old days" was much stronger among those away than among those who were caught up naturally in the changes as they occurred and knew that the "old days" no longer existed. And so, many practices and systems, which at home had long since changed with the times, remained unchanged abroad for a century. Yet they still seemed to represent progress to those whose point of reference was no longer progressive Europe but the primitive bush, and the indigenous population, even more removed from communication with developments abroad, took their standards from the only representatives of modern progress that they knew.

It is very difficult for the newer nations to throw off these influences completely, however disenchanted they may have become with the system in general. Although the present generation is in revolt against its colonial or other previous authorities, it comes from a tradition that defers to authority; although it has overthrown the political domination of the colonial powers, it is still under the influence of their symbols, rituals, and rules; thus the devotion to outmoded systems and routines, to ceremonies and protocol, to models and examples which derive from the very system they imagine they are repudiating. The revolution that is now taking place among the developing nations is hampered in many ways by the natural tendency to cling to the standards that have, after all, always represented progress.

Nor is it always an easy decision to make, between what should be rejected from the past and what should be retained as useful to the present and the future. One of the first moves in many of the newer countries, and one of the most detrimental to the achievement of most of their goals, has been the repudiation of the colonial language in favor of a native one. The motive is easy enough to understand; certainly any nation is justified in urging that its children know their own language before they learn the language of some foreign land. But in many of the developing countries, English (or at least one of the major European languages) is the only channel through which they can keep in touch with most of the latest developments in science, technology, and the social sciences.

We probably seldom think how important it has been in our own development that we had English as our working language when we threw off the yoke of colonialism and began our struggle to establish an independent nation. Compare the ease with which we could appropriate existing publication and merely add to it with the problems faced by many of today's new nations which can boast no written literature of their own and must start from scratch to create the necessary tools of education, information, and enlightenment. If education is one of the major keys to the progress they seek, then the books, journals, and other sources of current information in the major disciplines are essential. To all intents and purposes if they do not have a language in which there is a great deal of current publication, they do not have the tools of learning in the fields that affect them the most.

To use English merely as an example: defining the role that it shall play in a country whose major language is not English is extremely difficult. Many nations have recognized the need for English as a second language, and introduce it as a compulsory subject at about the level of the seventh grade. But because it is a second language, because it often has been relegated to an even lower status for a certain transitional period, and because, even if the language is accepted as an essential tool, the English-speaking foreigner is still not always welcome, instruction in English is far below the standard necessary to make it a functional language for the average student. More and more the colleges and universities are finding that the student who has learned his English in a native school from a native instructor is incapable of doing the reading necessary to support his advanced studies. Many of the universities use English as the medium of instruction even if the elementary and secondary schools do not, and certainly all of them recognize the need to use some textbooks or collateral readings in English. But many have found that the instructors themselves must lapse into the language of the country whenever it is really necessary to make a point and that very little of the assigned reading is done if it must be done in a language not native to the student. We should not be surprised, knowing at what level of competence most of our students operate in the foreign language they take in high school. But certainly we should be able to sympathize.

You may think it odd that it has taken me so long

to come around to mentioning a problem which normally looms largest in both our thinking and theirs when we attempt to assist a developing country: the economic. While it cannot be denied that economic factors are important, it is a prejudice of mine that most of the economic difficulties arise as a result of the other shaping forces we have been discussing and that to attempt to meet the problems of the developing countries only with money is not to meet them at all. While it is true that some of the countries are deprived by nature, most of them are rich in the natural and human resources that could be developed to produce a respectable contribution to the world's wealth, if to do so were a task to which the people wished to address themselves. More often than not, however, the country is what we call "backward" industrially, technologically, and economically because its traditions and its values lead it to seek other goals, and until there is a change in attitudes and concepts, mere economic aid will change almost nothing. Meanwhile, I think the people of these countries are quite right to consider carefully whether they do indeed wish to change their way of life in these areas. The problems, anxieties, troubles, and conflicts that we are willing to accept in order to have certain material advantages may be considered too high a price to pay by people from another culture who prize what we have lost more than they covet what we have gained.

To countries which pride themselves on their spiritual qualities, like many of those in the Far East, to adherents of religious doctrines which proclaim the insignificance of the material world, to believers in a philosophy which stresses acceptance as a virtue, the weight we give to material things, to getting ahead, and to change and reform is seen as a weakness, not a strength. And if it is true, as we so blithely inform them without being asked, that they *must* change their ways if they are ever going to reach the kind of life we live, they might well decide that we demand far too much and offer too little in return.

But sometimes the rejection of change is not as conscious as this. Sometimes the way we think is so alien to the way that another people thinks that we can never reach a meeting of the minds, with the best will in the world. I am thinking, for example, of a cast of mind which is typical in Latin America, and which the Latinos themselves refer to as their *más o menos* philosophy. *Más o menos* — "more or less" — really does define an approach and an attitude. In Latin America, a meeting starts more or less at ten o'clock; a man is more or less five feet, eight inches tall; an item costs two hundred cruzeiros — more or less. To the North American this is most frustrating. Either you are five feet, eight inches tall, or you are not; either the meeting is scheduled for ten, or it is not. How can you *más o menos* run trains, build bridges, keep business engagements, sign contracts?

Certainly it is true that where precision, accuracy, exact measurement, and punctuality are essential, the *más o menos* philosophy can cause delays, errors, and losses that adversely affect the efficiency of the entire operation. On the other hand, the quantitative precisionist is equally out of his depth when he must deal with areas where subtle, qualitative, intangible phenomena are involved. It becomes a matter of deciding what is most important in one's scale of values. That decision has been made by the Latin Americans over the years, and probably without conscious resolve. So too, has ours. The reconciliation of these two views of the world cannot be accomplished by the mere proffer of economic aid. We are back where we began: if you do not speak the same language, a community of discourse is difficult, and this applies to an area much broader than the tongue we speak.

Since, as we stated at the beginning, libraries are social agencies which reflect the society of which they are a part, it is to be expected that these social influences of which we have been speaking should be mirrored in the kinds of libraries that we find in the developing countries. In a society which restricts education, with all that the word implies of access to information, knowledge, and ideas, the role of the library is automatically restricted too. The concept of a free public library is in complete opposition to the idea that education is the privilege of the few, that individual effort cannot possibly lead to an improvement of one's lot, and that people deserve to remain wherever the accident of birth has happened to place them. To promote equal opportunity is not a goal

skill has been developed, leaving the new literate no opportunity to exercise and to perfect his newly acquired
talent. It seems incredible that well-intentioned teachers
and educators would deliberately whet an appetite they
had no intention of satisfying, but that is what has happened in literacy programs around the world, including
those in which we have been involved. There was a role
for the library here, but how can there be libraries, particularly popular or public libraries, if few or no books
are published in the language that the general public can
read? A program of indigenous publishing and of translation should be as much a part of a literacy campaign
as is the teaching of reading itself; without them, many
countries are discovering that the gains of the classroom
are almost immediately lost and that all of that effort has
ended up with almost as large an illiterate group as ever.

Still, there is a group with education, and it is constantly growing in numbers. How is it that they do not
demand the kind of services that books and libraries can
perform for them? We know from every study of reading
ever carried out in the United States that education is
the major correlate of reading and library use. But we
soon learn that it is not education per se, but the *kind* of
education that makes the difference. The system of education in most of the developing countries places its
emphasis upon unquestioning acceptance of professorial
authority, and that means that books have very little part
to play in the process. The lecture notes and the single
textbook suffice to see the student through most of his

academic career, and everything about the system tends to discourage rather than to encourage the habit of reading. The texts are dull and uninviting. Outside reading is seldom assigned. Unassigned reading, if it leads to independent ideas or ideas in conflict with the class lectures, will jeopardize the student's chances to move ahead. Since advancement is based absolutely on examinations all along the ladder from elementary school to advanced study in the university, since the examinations are designed to test the student's rote memory of the lectures rather than his knowledge of the subject, and since the purpose of the system is to reduce the numbers who will go on for higher studies rather than to maximize the opportunities, it is the unusual student indeed who would be motivated to use libraries for any other purpose than as a space in which to cram for the examinations.

Even at the universities this system prevails, and since the college student usually comes with no school or public libraries anywhere in his experience, he does not miss them. For the exceptional student who catches the fancy of his professor there is always the collection locked in the professor's office, from which selected books are doled out as part of the special privilege that accrues to those at the top.

By and large it is probably safe to say that the library services of all kinds, limited though they may be, are pretty well meeting the demands made upon them, and that many of them are a lot better than the use that is made of them. Where there is no habit of book use and no knowledge of what libraries can do, there is not likely to be enough of an audience, aware of its unmet needs, to force the schools, the universities, or the municipalities to provide a better service.

The restrictions on education, and the large segment of the population that is deprived of schooling beyond the earliest levels, obviously limit the number of potential library workers as well as of potential library users. The shortages of highly trained professional personnel are to be expected, since the small number of libraries and the limited professional demands made upon their staffs make librarianship a low-priority career field. Since the role of libraries is such a limited one, status is low, salaries are inadequate, support is insufficient, and opportunities are not rewarding enough to attract many students. Consequently it is difficult to justify schools of librarianship of sufficient quantity and quality to meet even the limited needs. And since so few trained librarians can be produced within the country, it becomes almost impossible to break the vicious circle.

But personnel shortages are equally serious below the professional level. Most of the library tasks which we designate as sub-professional and clerical require a certain minimum of education, but in most of the developing countries even that minimum is attained by very few. Such simple duties as filing book charges, reshelving books, distributing the mail — a myriad of routines which demand only the simplest skills of literacy — are beyond the competence of those who can be hired for the salaries that such jobs command. This means that there are certain kinds of library services and certain ways of handling procedures that are closed to other countries, at least for the time being. Open shelves, for example, are resisted for a great number of reasons, but no small consideration is the fact that an open-shelf system absolutely requires that the shelves be kept in order. But shelf-reading, which we provide for without giving it a second thought, is one of the skills that requires more education than the job can afford in most developing countries.

Where so few have any education at all, a real sellers' market develops. Anyone who has enough education to be able to handle the simple library jobs is too valuable to be spared for them. Government service, business, and technology need him too, and can pay him better. This is a problem all up and down the line in library work, and certainly the professionally trained librarian is obviously a potential candidate for responsibilities in agencies which carry greater prestige than does the library. Either he chooses a more prestigious field to begin with if he is willing to undertake as much schooling as librarianship requires, or he is lured away from it when his education is completed.

Prestige, important in any society, is especially crucial in a class-conscious one. Where a librarian in the United States, if he were faced with clerical staff shortages, might be quite willing to shelve books, carry packages, or even sweep the floor if that were the only way to keep the library functioning, most of the librarians in other countries could not risk the loss of face. Tasks which we hand over to a high school student on a part-time basis, or which are eagerly sought by our college students to help them pay their way through school, would not be touched by the students in many of the developing countries because they could not accept an assignment so inconsistent with the status conferred upon them by the mere fact that they are being educated. Not only will the educated refuse jobs which have tradition-ally been handled by lower-class persons; they are likely to resist any position which places them in direct contact with members of a lesser class or requires them to per-form a service for someone beneath them on the social scale. Translated into the hard but simple facts of our own professional life, this even means that there are qualified librarians who would never demean themselves by working in a library which serves the general public. It is as direct and as outspoken as that. The simpler, but essential, jobs of day-to-day library operations are thus frequently above the competence of the only people who would be content to perform them, and below the level of those qualified to handle them. And so, more often than not, they don't get done.

This strong drive to preserve status is reinforced — by tribal loyalties, by nationalism, by professional jeal-ousies — to militate against almost any kind of coopera-tive effort. It means a loss of face in some societies to act on the advice or recommendations of anyone else since this seems to indicate that you acknowledge the superiority of the other; it means a loss of social status in some cultures to be associated with people from another class; it means a loss of independence in still others to work in any kind of joint venture rather than alone, no matter what long-term benefits might accrue. The economics of the library situation would certainly seem to dictate that the most be made of what is available instead of multiplying the instances of costly duplication of resources and effort. Through cooperation, much that is not now possible with limited funds could be possible. But unfortunately there is a counter-tendency fostered by the economics of the situation. Where opportunities are few, every other person with similar qualifications and interests is much more urgently a potential rival. Each accomplishment by someone else spells a danger to one's own position in the scramble for advancement to the few good jobs that exist. Where such a situation prevails, it is considered merely foolhardy, not admirable, to subordinate one's own interests to some broader good.

Thus in most of the developing countries a library association does not exist at all, or if it does, it is almost completely ineffectual. The kind of cooperation, coordination, and acknowledged interdependence required to make group action effective is too alien to too many of the traditions. And therefore, many of the activities and services that we consider essential are difficult to introduce in the developing countries if they rest upon cooperative effort. The absence of union catalogs, union

[55]

lists of serials, national bibliographies, and so many other tools basic to the functioning of our libraries can be explained in part by this situation.

It is for this reason, and for many others connected with attitudes, usage, and customs, that I feel that outside economic aid is of secondary importance in effecting basic changes. Admittedly money is tight, foreign exchange is often nonexistent, and the costs of library service come high. But until the desire exists to provide a library service, local money will never be found and foreign money alone will not create it. It is usually the lack of real conviction rather than of dollars and cents that accounts for the limitations on service of which we have been speaking. Throughout all of the regions from which I have been gleaning my negative examples there are libraries that do perform services, do reflect modern concepts, and do present a positive picture. They are there because of individuals who knew what they wanted, and wanted it badly enough to work for it. They did not always have outside resources to support them, whereas many of the inadequate services did.

But if the lack of money does not keep the library concept from coming into being, it can hamper its fullest implementation. The purchase of books and equipment, the building of appropriate quarters, the provision of adequate salaries all require money. And where money and materials are in short supply, limitations may have to be placed on services which affect the very purpose of the library. The shortage of books, the high costs of the books that do exist, and the delays and difficulties involved where books must be bought from abroad at prices geared to an entirely different economy help to account in part for the emphasis upon preservation and protection which characterizes library practice in so many countries abroad. I have mentioned the principle of "personal accountability" whereby the librarian is required to account for every book in the inventory, and to pay, out of his own pocket, for any book missing at the time of the annual book count. To those who believe that the reader is more important than the book, this system is unacceptable. Nothing could be better designed to force libraries to place their books under lock and key, to refuse to circulate them, and to devise all manner of restrictions upon use. "Can't they see," the American librarian wonders, "that books will always remain locked up under such a system?" Of course they can; the locked case is not an unforeseen result of the system; it is its purpose. Even in our allegedly open-shelf libraries we lock up those books that are rare, extremely costly, difficult to replace, or likely to be stolen. In a country where any book is rare, costly, difficult to replace, or likely to be stolen, all of the books are locked up, and the man in charge of the books — the librarian — must be made responsible. The business of the librarian inevitably becomes the preservation of books rather than their dissemination. And this predisposition is so well established that even where book collections or money to buy them are made available from outside sources, these books merely go into locked cases too, and the expenditure has no influence at all on accessibility or service.

Not all of the differences are psychological or economic. Obviously there are some natural conditions that alter the capability of a country or a people to sustain some of the activities which underlie the concept of library service which we hold. It is not merely coincidental that so many of the developing countries lie in the tropical zone. The heat, the humidity, the torrential rains, the enervating climates of many of these countries impose a limitation upon activity and a drain upon energy that make it impossible to carry on at the pace that comes naturally in more temperate areas. There are also countries whose soil will not sustain the food necessary to build a strong and energetic people. This is not just a matter of insufficient food; it is also a matter of food insufficiently rich in the properties that make for health and vitality. Against such difficulties it is not enough to demand that the people make up their minds to change. On the other hand, means are now available to make it possible for man to exercise more control over his environment. It really is — or will soon be — a matter of education and interest much more than of latitude and longitude. Already we have seen deserts blossom and harsh lands soften, where the will to have them do so has been present.

There are other phenomena, natural to the culture, which impose certain barriers against some of the solutions which come naturally to us. A simple example is that of the language with which the country works, and which shapes its thinking. Nonalphabetical languages, like Chinese, for example, not only do not lend themselves to an alphabetical arrangement, they impose a different kind of logic which alters the way the people approach the basic problems of library organization. Our tendency to put things in a-b-c order is a good example of the "natural" way of doing things which is natural only where certain conditions obtain. Since the filing of Chinese cannot employ the alphabetic principle, more than one other "natural" way has been devised to arrange a Chinese-language catalog. One such method is by the number of strokes in a character, and I have seen a library patron writing out the character in the palm of his hand to determine how many strokes are involved before approaching the card catalog. This strikes us as odd, but it is no stranger than our method of mentally going through a piece of the alphabet — l-m-n-o-p — before we start our alphabetical search. When an ideographic language is combined with a complicated usage of personal names, as in the Orient, our whole system of bibliographic organization and cataloging practice becomes irrelevant. A personal name as main entry is not the logical first approach if a man's name changes several times throughout his lifetime, or if custom dictates the use not of his family name but of some other. To those of us brought up on the ALA Rules, a catalog that is not in alphabetical order and that does not use the author's last name as a main entry seems to be a shambles, but the real shambles ensues not so much when our rules are ignored as when they are forced upon a situation for which they are unsuited.

These are mere details, of course, but they illustrate the kind of trap into which we tend to fall when we bring our own solutions to other people's problems. Many of the procedural difficulties faced in foreign libraries were compounded by the assistance we have given through our instruction and advice. Our teachers have taught rules, and have either failed to stress the need for adaptations or have assumed that they would, of course, be made as needed. But adaptation or rejection of what is taught would be an affront to the dignity and authority accorded the professor, and flies in the face of the tradition. The fault lies not with the student who did not make all the necessary adjustments, but with the teacher who failed to understand that he was asking the student to perform the psychologically impossible.

To define more clearly the point at which so many of our misunderstandings occur, I will have to borrow a term from the educationists. The difference can be identified by the distinction which must be recognized between a need and a *felt* need. Over and over again, the distance between two concepts of a service, an objective, or a procedure can be measured by the gap that exists between what each faction sees as the essentials. The essentials are determined by the goals each side wishes to attain, whether overtly stated or not. And the goals reflect the system of values each party holds, determined by its history, its tradition, its culture. We are as much victims of our heredity and environment as they are of theirs, and if your reaction to that statement is, in essence, "Yes, but we've come up with the more sensible answers," you only prove the point. It is very difficult for any of us, on either side of the world, to weigh, measure, or evaluate on scales we do not know how to use.

This conclusion is not meant to be discouraging. It is a hard fact that understanding and communication across cultures are difficult, but that does not mean they are impossible, or that they are not worth attempting. A realistic recognition of the problem gives us our best chance to make the first step toward its solution; the situation becomes hopeless only when we fail to realize that there is a problem, or refuse to face it. We of the United States have been guilty of both of these errors in our past efforts to aid the developing countries in almost every area of endeavor, including librarianship. There have been many failures, and false starts, and wild goose chases, and dead ends. We will look at some of them in the next chapter, which deals with the role of American librarianship. But let me anticipate its concluding conviction that we do, nevertheless, have a role. The attempt made here not merely to describe what others do but also to understand why they do it is in the nature of essential rehearsal for the part American librarianship can play in the unfolding drama of the developing nations.

III

The Role of
American
Librarianship

At the end of the preceding chapter I tried to suggest
that the cast of my remarks — the emphasis on differences and the conditions that cause them — is only apparently negative, but not really so. If one contemplates
building a bridge across a chasm, it is only sensible to try
to determine all of the factors that may affect eventual

had some outstanding successes, and some very disappointing failures. Many of the latter might well have been avoided if the simple bridge-builder questions had been asked. Does anyone really want to cross at this point? Are they prepared to pay what it costs to construct the best bridge for the purpose? Are the necessary tools available? Will it be maintained once it is built? Does the fact that we have built some good bridges in our own country necessarily qualify us for taking on the job in unfamiliar terrain and with unfamiliar materials?

Perhaps the hardest of all the questions to answer is the first: does anyone really want the help we offer? It is hard to answer because neither we nor they really know. More often than not, outside experts are called in because the developing country really believes it wants to introduce libraries, or change the nature of its traditional ones. What it does not know is how much is involved in such a development — in time, in money, in effort, and more important than these, in challenge to basic concepts. I have hinted at a few of these in the preceding chapter and have tried to suggest that until the concepts change, the other factors are of secondary importance. You *can* change human nature, but it is a much harder, slower, and more involved process than we usually imagine. It is seldom accomplished in the course of a nine-month Fulbright assignment, or a three-year AID contract, or the duration of a foundation grant, generous though they might be in time, effort, and money. A start can sometimes be made within the time limits, but the abrupt halt to which these projects come when the term ends continues to plague these endeavors.

The shortage of time is a problem not only for the local librarians, but for the visiting one as well. It takes longer to get things done, for a variety of reasons, and some of them are inevitable. When one is overseas, he is, well, overseas. To get books or materials is not merely a matter of telephoning the local wholesaler or putting through an order for delivery within the next few days, or even weeks. The visiting professor who arrives in time to teach his first semester class only to discover that the books he needs are not available is not likely to get them before the semester is over. Air mail is prohibitively expensive for such weights at such distances; sea mail is a matter of six months on the average. These are delays which are nobody's fault; they cannot be corrected even by a change of heart or mind.

But the heart and mind changes are far more important and they may require not months, but years. And what must not be forgotten is that our preconceptions are just as much involved as theirs, and that there is resistance to change or adjustment on our side too. Typically any outside expert, when he is called in to offer the benefits of his expertise, assumes that he has been chosen in order to bring with him the institutions, attitudes, and techniques on which he is an expert. It is a natural enough reaction, a natural enough mistake.

"Mistake" because, as I cannot repeat too often, the solutions that work in one cultural milieu do not necessarily work in another. We have brought in the Dewey Decimal System, a classification which even in its latest, more flexible editions is still inadequate for the areas in which the greatest amount of publication is likely to take place abroad — in the literature, the history, the philosophy, and the religion of the country. We advocate the use of LC cards, forgetting how little of a foreign library's collection will consist of the titles, let alone the editions, which the cards represent. We introduce our subject headings, overlooking the fact that languages are not made up merely of different words, but of different concepts and approaches. We order electrical equipment where there is little or no electricity; we purchase book-mobiles where there are no roads; we donate the out-dated discards from our own collections to countries that need the latest information but cannot read English.

These failures to identify key differences in the environments could be corrected, of course. Concrete matters like these are not too difficult to ascertain, and with a little time and a little experience, many of these mistakes would not be made. It is much harder to learn, even when one is on the scene, about less tangible factors like social taboos, traditional practices, and inbred prejudices. And the short-term visiting expert is usually required to make certain basic decisions immediately — often even before he arrives on the foreign scene — and with the best of intentions he cannot be expected to know all he needs to know.

These problems arise for any outside expert, not only

for the American. Do not let such oversimplified accounts as that in *The Ugly American* fool you into believing that somehow we are so much less effective abroad than are the representatives of other countries. The simple truth is bad enough: we are not any better. But we are learning, which is more than can be said for many of the others.

What we share with the others is our status as foreigners, inevitable whenever we are in another country, but sometimes difficult for us to accept. Whatever we might have to offer comes from outside and to that extent may be just a bit suspect, just a bit unwelcome. In our own eyes our intentions are so pure, our integrity so certain, our selflessness so apparent, our technical knowledge so superior that we find it difficult to believe that anyone could, for a moment, question our motives, suspect our ability, or consider another alternative. We do not think of ourselves in political terms when we offer professional assistance to libraries, but the political implications are always in the minds of our hosts. Our protestations that we have no motivation other than pure altruism and professional commitment must contend with the incontrovertible fact that history, both ours and theirs, argues against so innocent an intention. The Russians, the British, the French all have their axes to grind; is it believable that somehow the Americans do not? We are all lumped together, and our aims and methods are seen as essentially indistinguishable. In many of these countries, the term "European" includes the Americans, and while we are not any more suspect than any other foreign group, we are assumed to have a bill of goods to sell like all the others.

There are other complications as well. It must be remembered that what we consider to be a benefaction may well merely mean additional problems for the receiver. A large grant of money, the donation of a building, a gift collection of books, or the establishment of a service all require that something be done about them. We have found this to be true in our own country; the addition of a gift book to the collection is not cost-free; the administration of a grant is not without its price in time, staff, and money. In some cases we cannot afford to accept gifts either, because of the drain upon time, staff, and facilities they entail. It should not surprise us as much as it always seems to do that the intended recipients of our assistance are not always quick to accept, or grateful to receive. There are invariably some kind of strings attached, if not always political ones.

As a case in point, let us explore a bit the problems involved in sending a student to the United States for his library training. On the surface it would appear that the opportunity to study abroad would be an ideal solution for those countries which do not yet have their own library training programs, or programs at a level advanced enough to prepare for positions of leadership. Yet many countries are extremely cautious about approving such training, and suspicious of their value even where scholarships and fellowships cover the costs. I am not here speaking of the adjustments that must be made by the individual — to separation from home and family and to unfamiliar climate, customs, food, language, and teaching method. Generally speaking, the individual student welcomes the opportunity, and all of us who have been connected with American library schools can attest to the avidity of students from abroad to take advantage of any opportunity for an American educational experience that comes their way. I am speaking rather of the official attitude of the government and the professional leaders of foreign countries who must decide whether or not to give permission to the eager student to travel abroad for his professional education.

A first concern is that the overseas experience, especially for the young or immature student, will contribute to a kind of denationalization which could be harmful. The education he receives in the United States is American education, built around American practice and American objectives. The student who is not sufficiently mature or flexible to distinguish between what is applicable and what is not may well be alienated from his own culture, and could return with ideas and expectations completely unsuited to the aims and the capacities of his native land. He may expect a recognition and a status which has not yet been achieved in his own country; he begins to be accustomed to facilities and equipment which cannot yet be provided; he looks for a response from users and a support from the community which it is his task to develop rather than to find already flourishing.

Like the country boy brought to the big city, he may find himself not quite attuned to the new life but forever spoiled for the old.

In such cases, the returnee librarian makes little or no contribution to the development of librarianship in his own country, but finds himself so frustrated by thwarted expectations that he may leave the profession and even the country the first time an opportunity presents itself. Study abroad, as a matter of fact, is a well-known back door to emigration, and there is an understandable concern over the gamble introduced whenever the brighter and more promising young people are sent away. Indeed, there is some resistance to sending the best in any case, since this deprives the home country of their talents for a year or two or more, at the very time that they might best be used to sharpen the minds of their fellow students and colleagues. Yet it makes no sense to send other than the best for advanced training designed to prepare for leadership.

The alternative to overseas training is not really available in many of the developing nations at the present time, and the establishment of a library school in the home country is not the easy solution it may at first appear. The essentials of good library education are seldom present where librarianship and publishing are still in their early stages. The fact that there are no library schools in the country means that there are few people with the kind of qualifications needed by a teacher at the appropriate level for professional education. The likelihood is that there will be few basic books of librarianship in the language of the country, and that books in English (which is the language of most of the major texts and professional tools) will not be read with sufficient facility to make them useful in instruction. Translations, on the other hand, seldom justify the time, cost, and effort they require because almost any foreign book to be of real use in the teaching situation will have to be re-written, adapted, and edited to meet local needs. Good libraries are seldom available as models or as laboratories. Practice work, which is an essential where the student has had no previous opportunity to use libraries, will not offer the kind of experience which will lead to improvement in library services or to the stimulation of standards toward which to strive. There is much to be said for library education on the home ground rather than in another country, but not if it must be so far below standard as to offer no contribution to the advancement of the profession or of library service.

Foreign aid and technical assistance have been the devices we have used to attack these difficulties, with technical assistance usually seen as the provision of a qualified teacher from outside the country, since no well-trained people are to be found within it. But the visiting instructor is as hampered by the local conditions as the native teacher would be, and once again we face the additional problems of the short-term appointment, the period of adjustment, the failure to understand local needs and values, and the difficulties of language.

There seems to be no simple and unassailable panacea.

There is another very real concern that has troubled thoughtful people on both sides of any aid transaction: does outside assistance stifle local initiative and substitute foreign for indigenous effort? The professed purpose of external financing is to provide the "seed money," the pump priming, the initial impetus that will start things going. If the concept is new, or the technique different from what is now known in the country, the assistance from outside will serve to introduce it so that it can be carried on by the country itself. But many of our experiences abroad have shown that the libraries and the library techniques that we introduce are not taken up as models, even where the demonstration has been the purpose of the installation, as in some of the UNESCO pilot libraries, for example. The most that can be said is that demonstration libraries stimulate requests for more outside assistance, reflecting internal rivalries and jealousies much more than they do any real interest in the library as a library.

The evidence seems to show that where models have been provided, like, for example, the USIS and British Council libraries, the local community generally sees no need to introduce its own, and local support then goes for other things. This discourages librarians who like to think that once a good library service is demonstrated, an overwhelming public demand for more will be kindled. But here we must recognize the political implications of our overseas libraries. The primary aim of the USIS library is not the promotion of library service as such, but the dissemination of favorable information about the United States. Thus when a mob attacks a USIS library, it is a protest in the political sphere, and when the library is destroyed or put out of commission, the local government is not inclined (nor urged by a book-hungry public) to put up a replacement library of its own. What they have destroyed, in their eyes, is not a library service but an agency of American propaganda; hence, there is no need whatsoever to replace it.

And, of course, they are not completely wrong: it is to our interest politically to have the USIS library there to serve our purposes, and after a suitable token protest, we can be counted on to replace the books and the library as a tool of our foreign policy. From the professional point of view it is unfortunate that the best examples of American library service should be so inextricably bound up with foreign politics in the minds of the people overseas, but it is a fact of life, and I am convinced that it does in part inhibit the acceptance of our philosophy of library service. Nor is our situation helped much by the fact that similar information libraries from Russia, Germany, France, and many other countries line up, in a sense, along the same street to reinforce the suspicion that a public library — any public library — is a special-interest, brain-washing agency rather than an institution of disinterested education.

As a matter of fact, the single street of rival information centers actually exists in some places, and figuratively exists in all of them. The resistance that American method and American practice encounter abroad may even be, frequently, much less from the host country than from the other foreign presences. The colonial power that was recently in control, of course, is especially resistant to change because it has had a long time to settle in. This is indeed part of the reason for the resistance; in Africa, for example, the Americans are really late-comers on the scene, who now attempt to capitalize on the years of work, attention, and devotion that other countries have put into Africa to build its cities, develop its institutions, and provide whatever modern education now exists. If we suggest that such attention from the British, the French, the Portuguese, the Belgians, and others was not exactly a purely altruistic one, I assure you that our sudden interest is viewed as something less than selfless too. The Africans suspect that our concern is much less with helping Africa than with shoring up our own defenses and investments against rival powers, and none of the former colonials is likely to let slip the opportunity to make the most of that ready-made anti-American weapon.

Understandably, the nations which have been under the influence of a colonial power for the past several generations tend to find their models in the nation they know best. A former French colony looks to France, a British one to Britain, for its standards and criteria. When the University of Algiers began to rebuild after its destruction by the departing French, it sought to re-create the

Algerian Sorbonne that it had always been. This would seem to us to be the ideal occasion to introduce the open stacks, the classified arrangement, the circulation and reference systems which the French university system had never accommodated. But the Algerians have no such intention. Our provincial notion that everybody really wants our kind of free and open library is quite mistaken. The American model is seen as inferior to the French—as indeed it may be to serve a system of French education.

I have spoken before of the continuing influence of the colonial traditions, and anyone who hopes to introduce American method and forms into former colonial areas must be familiar with the existing system and its values for the country. Often when we find something that strikes us as alien or outmoded in library practice in a developing country, we tend to imagine that it reflects a fumbling, primitive, and unlettered attempt to create a service without sufficient professional background to do it right. More often than not, it turns out that this "underdeveloped" approach comes directly from a highly developed country where it is still the standard. One can hardly call the British and French universities underdeveloped or ineffective, yet their library habits are frequently tied to practices centuries old. The American comes in firmly convinced — or at least loudly protesting — that there can be no decent education without wide and free use of books, good libraries open to student use, and reference and bibliographical services which characterize the most liberal ideal of American librarianship. The unvarnished truth of the matter is that there is very good higher education in the European tradition and it would be foolish to deny it. Yet the closed-stack, difficult-to-use, locked-office tradition remains standard in many of the great European universities. Our insistence that this militates against good education is not particularly persuasive, especially to a society that is already conditioned to a system that is based upon the European tradition. How is it that we are apparently so wrong in our conviction?

The answer, of course, lies in the kind of education one wants. The European tradition of which we speak, and which is beginning to change in some places, is that which reserves higher education for a very small elect who have been able to run the gamut of elimination examinations. By the time a student has qualified for the university, he is a member of a very limited group, well attuned to the particular kind of academic life he will have to lead. Under the special tutelage of some professor who likes him or to whom he demonstrates a particular talent, he receives the kind of individual attention which makes available to him the books and selected readings that the professor has gathered up in his private locked collection. The stress is placed on highly concentrated specialization, not broad, general education in our sense. He comes out a deep, but presumably narrower, scholar.

But he is a scholar, and he usually has acquired a

love of books despite the fact that stacks are closed, catalogs are uninformative, and library service is limited. The cost of such education, however, is the loss of many good students who may not qualify for this highly specialized kind of scholarship, or who may not have been able to demonstrate it early enough. The students who do come through such a system are likely to be the superior ones. But how many good-to-excellent ones have been lost along the route? The question that the developing nations must ask themselves is whether they can afford to lose the talents of so many people at this urgent point in the national development. The American prejudice is that they cannot, that the best route to rapid development is the widest utilization of all the talent available. But it must be admitted that there is at least a debatable point here, and that those who advocate education for leadership rather than broad training for everyone can make a rather convincing case. If the developing nations opt for capitalizing on as wide a range of talents as can be identified, the broader, popular, public library approach will support them in their search; if they decide instead that a small, select elite is more urgently needed, the library in the aristocratic tradition will serve adequately enough.

And so we are led to the all-important question: what exactly do we in America have to offer the developing nations that will help them to generate the kinds of libraries, librarians, and library services best suited to their needs and their aspirations? In spite of all the difficulties I have been enumerating throughout this book, I think we do have something — and something important. The canyon is deep and the chasm is wide, but that is all the more reason to believe that a good bridge is needed. And the Americans have built some excellent bridges.

This question has already been explored with care and insight by Dr. Raynard Swank when he was Director of the International Relations Office. In his excellent paper, "International Values in American Librarianship,"[1] he enumerated six characteristics of American librarianship that he felt were suitable for export, and since his analysis was so cogent I should like to borrow most of his concepts and elaborate only a little with some additional notes of my own.

The six characteristics which Dr. Swank enumerated are: (1) the conception of the library as an organization of books, (2) the evolution of a library profession, (3) the attitude of service, (4) the function of the library as an educational institution, (5) the role of the library in the advancement of intellectual freedom, and (6) the conception of organized information as a public resource and responsibility. Before I deal specifically with the individual characteristics he has identified, I should like to comment on a more general characteristic which forms the philosophical base on which these others rest. This

[1] Raynard C. Swank, "International Values in American Librarianship," in *The Cornell Library Conference,* Papers Read at the Dedication of the Central Libraries, October, 1962, Ithaca, N.Y., Cornell University Library, 1964, pp. 115-129.

is our concept of education itself. The role that the library — including the public library — can play in promoting, supporting, extending, and enriching formal education is determined very largely by the nature of that education. I have already identified my American bias in favor of a kind of education which attempts to provide an opportunity on several levels and for several kinds of qualifications, rather than one which presents an obstacle course designed to eliminate all but a very few. This view of education seems to me to be a valuable one for the developing countries where so much needs to be done on so many fronts in such a short time. All of the available talent should be used to the top of its capacity; the wastage of large numbers of useful people through a system designed to identify losers rather than to encourage winners seems to me to be a much less utilitarian form to follow. And when Dr. Swank speaks of the organization of books for use, of the attitude of service, of the function of the library as an educational institution, of the conception of organized information as a natural resource — even of the library's role in the advancement of intellectual freedom — he is speaking within the context of the kind of open and free educational system in which these concepts of the library can flourish. It is discouraging but realistic to recognize that the library cannot do much of this by itself, if the idea of education and its aims continues to cling to a tradition in which books, libraries, and freedom of access have no place.

[79]

As Dr. Swank points out in his paper,[2] ". . . only within the last century, and particularly in the United States and Great Britain, has the idea grown that the library should become a collection of books organized for efficient use. . . ." It has already been remarked how frequently the organization of books in libraries is one which bears no relation to ease of use. If libraries are to play a part in the development of the emerging nations, they will have to add to their objective of preservation that of utilization of the knowledge and ideas that rest within the books. To view the book simply as an artifact is legitimate enough but not if books and libraries are to have any kind of dynamic impact upon the developing society. Organization for efficient use, with its emphasis upon speed and ease of access, is peculiarly, if not exclusively, characteristic of American library development, which has something valuable to offer other societies besides our own.

Such a concept of the library leads logically into the characteristic which Swank has identified as the attitude of service. As he points out, "the attitude is no different from that of physicians, ministers, and members of other professions who are dedicated to their social missions. It is simply the attitude of helpfulness, the motive of being useful to other people . . . service is the cardinal principle of American librarianship."[3] To see the library as a "utilitarian device to further the general welfare" is to

[2] *Ibid.,* pp. 117-118.
[3] *Ibid.,* p. 122.

make it a vital part in the forward march of the society as a whole; without such a concept, the library is merely an appendage without purpose, a vestigial holdover which could be removed without loss to the functioning of the society. Thus here again we have a concept which is useful, not because it is American, but because it contributes to the progress of the developing nations.

"It is probable," says Dr. Swank, "that the libraries of no country other than the United States, except the Soviet Union, have been so clearly conceived as playing a positive role in the life-long education of all the people."[4] Note the assumption here, which Swank says is "common knowledge of course," that "books and reading are central to learning." I wish I could agree with that "of course," but we have already seen how uncommon the concept is in many systems of education in other countries. The function of the library as an educational institution is one that is tied to the idea that education should be made available to all of the people to the extent that they have the capacity to use it. It capitalizes upon the strengths of the library to speak to a great variety of potentialities and capabilities. If the developing countries are serious in their expressed intention to accelerate the improvement of the people, the library could be a most useful tool. The values of the concept of the library as an educational institution could be universal, not merely American or Russian.

To the nation that is moving ahead on many fronts,

[4] *Ibid.*, p. 123.

telescoping into a few decades what it has taken the developed countries a couple of centuries to accomplish, it is necessary to come to the realization that "the totality of recorded knowledge, collected, controlled and analyzed intellectually for use, is itself a public resource that is vital even to the welfare of nations."[5] This idea is related to the others that have gone before it; it proclaims that information is not just the private concern of an educated elite but also a significant public concern. It requires the kind of education that is open to that broader public, and the kinds of libraries that can control recorded knowledge in an orderly way to serve it. Many nations have begun to accept this concept, at least in science and technology, but it applies equally to the humanities and the social sciences as well. It is not an American idea alone, but the United States is certainly one of the leaders in implementing it most fully.

For all of these reasons, or perhaps better, for all of these facets of the overarching reason, American librarianship does have that which is useful and adaptable to the developing nations. Our willingness to experiment, innovate, and move with the times fits in perfectly with the desires of the new nations. Our demonstrated efficiency in many of the newer fields of bibliographical control and information retrieval provides the costly experimentation which the new nations cannot afford but the results of which they can utilize. The ferment on the social front in our country has opened up areas for inves-

[5] *Ibid.*, p. 127.

tigation and action of vital significance to the developing nations. Our anti-poverty program, our concern with newly literate adults, our extension of services to rural areas, our experiments with cooperative systems, our development of machines and nonbook devices to serve library purposes, our attempts to upgrade our school libraries, our effort to give service to students through all kinds of library agencies, our constant work to improve textbooks and other books for children, all of these are teaching us things that the developing countries also want to know. These are no longer the problems of a wealthy and well-favored nation remote from the problems of the rest of the world; in librarianship, the United States can be said also to be, still, a developing country. And, because these are universal rather than local problems, there can be a real exchange of knowledge and learning, not only from us to them, but from them to us. This is the useful exchange that was identified at the beginning of Chapter I. It is, in the long run, the real aim of international library relations.

What must we do to promote this more fruitful exchange? What can we do that we are not already doing — or at least trying to do? First of all, I think, we must begin to see ourselves as an equal partner in an exchange rather than as a condescending Lady Bountiful. We must, as the 1965 White House Conference on International Cooperation phrased it, develop an Ear of America as well as a Voice. We must listen as well as tell, learn as well as teach, receive as well as give. It is true that we have much more material wealth than the developing nations have and that we have had more years of experience in dealing with our own library problems at a professional level. But this does not mean that we have nothing to learn from other practices, or other proposed solutions. Until we really believe that — not just say that we do — we create an unfavorable atmosphere in which to carry on the exchange from which we both might benefit so much.

Second, we must recognize, much more tangibly than we now do, the need for other countries to adapt rather than to adopt the methods and procedures that we happen to favor for our own purposes. There are two important places where this recognition must be demonstrated: one, of course, is in any foreign assignment we take, whether short-term or long, where we have the opportunity to introduce American practice and offer American expertise. The other is in our teaching both here and abroad, where foreign students, or American students who may one day accept an overseas assignment, are introduced to the concepts that underlie library service. This suggests a reform in American education for librarianship quite apart from its particular application to the training of librarians from overseas. It indicates the need to accomplish, much better than we have yet done, the teaching of principles rather than rules, and a shift of emphasis away from how-to to why and what for.

I am not here advocating that we temper our programs of library education to spare the poor shorn lamb from another country. I am really suggesting that we raise our standards rather than lower them. The purpose of the foreign student who comes to the United States is to be exposed to American education; if we order the program to reflect only the highly specialized needs of his own country, he would do a lot better to take his training at home. We do him no favor to give him a watered-down program. We do not help librarianship in his home country by sending him back with below-standard education. And we harm the reputation of American education by permitting second-rate training to represent us abroad.

On the other hand, there is the problem of the foreign student whose overseas education has been so narrowly tied to American practice and expectations that he is unfitted for the task of building the kind of library service his country needs and can use. I would therefore urge that our upgraded program emphasize the need to adapt basic principles to specific purposes and conditions and demand of the student that he reach his own conclusions based upon a consideration of all the relevant factors. This will require him to analyze and to think, not just to listen and to repeat. It will result in an understanding of the rules deep enough to permit their relaxation or even abandonment for appropriate reason, and it will train him to formulate adaptations that will preserve the purpose of the rule wherever it has value. I submit that this is as important for the American student as it is for the student from another country.

This kind of teaching is harder for all concerned. It will demand more of the teacher as well as of the student. And it will be particularly difficult for the foreign student who must struggle with additional problems of adjustment and language. Which suggests, of course, that we may have to be much more strict in our screening of applicants from other countries. If the student does not have the background he needs to carry our courses, he must get it; we should not dilute our courses on his account. If the applicant lacks sufficient proficiency in the language to carry the load of reading, writing, and class participation that our courses demand, he is not yet ready to enter our program. This is a tough policy, but it is the only one that will accomplish the aims that both the foreign student and the American teacher profess. It will eliminate some of the students who today are creating the most serious problems for us, and for their home countries upon their return. As for the better students, it may defer but need not eliminate those who will truly benefit themselves and the profession of librarianship.

This tighter control on admission should be welcomed abroad, for it would more surely screen out the immature and undiscriminating student who is most likely to be seduced by the glamour of a rich country. The more mature student can select more sensibly that which is applicable and that which is not; he is likely to be more committed to his own country and its needs; he will hopefully be more serious about the professional part of his American visit and less inclined to be diverted by irrelevant attractions. There is no way absolutely to insure that the student will return to his own country or remain there if he does return; some of this does not rest with us to determine in any case. Until there is better recognition of professional qualifications and better opportunity to use his talents, the good librarian is inevitably going to be lured away by the chance to use his training instead of waste it. But the attrition is probably greater than it should be, and a better selection at the beginning might help to eliminate some of those for whom admission to an American library school is merely a means for getting the trip or escaping from home.

Better and more careful selection of Americans who go overseas is also needed. There is just as much interest in a free trip from here to there as there is from there to here. The person who takes on the responsibility of an overseas assignment should be one who recognizes the seriousness and the importance of the task, who is willing to accept a commitment to a longer period abroad, who acknowledges the fact that he will have to make adjustments not only in his physical comforts but in his habits of thought and work. This calls for changes not only in the individual, but in institutional attitudes as well. The difficulties and frustrations Americans have faced on overseas assignments have come as much from the policies and procedures of our American agencies as from any cultural clashes abroad. I need not here repeat the criticisms enumerated by John Gardner in his report to the Agency for International Development.[6] Although they are directed specifically at AID's relations with universities, most of them apply equally to the problems of librarians serving on temporary assignment overseas, whether on an AID contract or under other auspices. I wish merely to commend the continuing and serious review of American policy which they have introduced. Too many appointments are made hurriedly and without sufficient care to meet some arbitrary American deadline like the imminent close of a budget period, or the schedule of the annual meeting of the board. Too many assignments serve a political purpose rather than a professional one. Too many are perfunctory — ill-supported and poorly planned — reflecting an indifference and a lack of concern at the top that cannot but affect the performance of the visiting expert. And too many are short-term and terminal, with no follow-up, no continuing review, and no evaluation of performance and results.

Especially if American librarians are going to be asked to spend longer periods abroad, there must be sufficient financial support and protection to justify the costs, not only in time and money, but in separation from American professional contacts and developments which affect one's future career. American librarians have shown a willingness to offer their assistance even when it

---

[6] John W. Gardner, "A.I.D. and the Universities; Report to the Administrator of the Agency for International Development," Washington, D.C., Agency for International Development, 1964.

means, as it often does, financial and personal sacrifice. But there are limits beyond which such sacrifices cannot be expected, especially if there is no real evidence that the supporting agency attaches much importance to the task. There must be more enlightened and serious attention paid by our own government to its overseas obligations at this level, more planning and less expediency, more selection of suitable people for the assignment and less filling the vacancies with anybody that happens to be available on split-second call, better definition of the level and the quality of the needed personnel as reflected in salaries, benefits, and conditions of employment.

There are other areas where our own government needs to review its present policies. One of our most important contributions could be to promote the free flow of information and materials through the passage of legislation to implement the Florence and Beirut Agreements.

Another would be to establish a central clearing-house to which libraries and scholars from abroad could apply for copies of needed materials. Present regulations, staff shortages, and other problems hamper the Library of Congress in its attempt to fulfill this function properly, and the United States, which should lead the world in the liberal provision of up-to-date information on the findings of research and scholarship, has a poor reputation throughout the scholarly world for the delays and difficulties which we now unavoidably place in the way.

A third would be the reinstatement of AID assistance to the United States Book Exchange, which was allowed to lapse through an unfortunate series of irrelevant circumstances. The United States Book Exchange system of providing materials to overseas libraries is one of the most valuable and least costly of all our endeavors in this field, and has benefited innumerable libraries both abroad and at home.

A fourth would be to find ways to assist publishers, both American and foreign, in schemes to make good original works and needed translations available at prices people can afford to pay.

It should be made clear that none of these ideas is new and that the government is already exploring all of them. The President has strongly urged in more than one message to Congress the implementation of the Florence and Beirut Agreements. The Library of Congress has indicated its willingness to take over the centralized clearinghouse function, and proposals have been made to the Agency for International Development for support. AID has itself embarked on an intensified book and translation program. But none of these has yet achieved the importance and the status required to give them the full support and attention they need to proceed rapidly and efficiently.

I should like also to see a serious review of USIA policy concerning the role of its overseas libraries. At present they are merely one device, along with radio, television, and traveling vaudeville shows, for bringing a picture of America to the people of other countries. The major criterion of success seems to be the size of the audience attracted. Quite apart from the unfair competition imposed between a "slow" medium like a book and a "fast" medium like a jazz concert, there is another subtle difference in presentation that deserves consideration. When a Louis Armstrong, a Jerome Robbins ballet, or an American lecturer is presented, it sells Americanism not directly, but indirectly by demonstrating an American accomplishment as it has been developed in the United States. The accomplishment is allowed to speak for itself. But the USIS Library is not permitted to demonstrate the American public library idea, which is one of our really great and unique inventions. Instead, the USIS Library is only permitted to sell directly. It may stock only American books by American authors on American themes—and even these are carefully screened (the impolite word is censored) to eliminate any which are deemed to be too critical or insufficiently favorable. The American library abroad is not an American library but a center for American propaganda, and in several overseas posts I have been told by the administrative officer that the library "is too much a library," meaning that the librarian has tried to give American library service instead of concentrating on more immediately measurable public relations activities.

I should like to suggest that even if we were to hold strictly to the State Department objective, we would accomplish our aims better by letting the rest of the world see a real American library rather than the library

of selected Americana which now represents us abroad.
Would we not create a better, and truer, picture of the
United States if we were the one library in Addis Ababa
or Rio or Bangkok to which a reader could go for real
general library service, instead of being merely one of
several foreign propaganda centers, no better, no worse,
no different from those of Russia, or Germany, or the
United Arab Republic? If, as Dr. Swank suggests, the
role of the library in the advancement of intellectual
freedom is one characteristic of American librarianship
worthy of emulation abroad, we are doing less than we
could with our USIS libraries to demonstrate it.

In all of these recommendations there is seen the
need for clearer understanding of the potentialities of the
book and of libraries. The failure to provide reading material to support programs of literacy is a glaring example
of a typical failure in many programs abroad, whether
supported by private or governmental funds. Large-scale
projects of university expansion have been underwritten,
often containing no provision for concurrent library development. Where libraries have been given some recognition, it is often as an afterthought, tacked on as a token
and obviously seen as an incidental rather than an integral part of the major program. And even when the
library is the central object of support, the planning and
implementation all too frequently reveal an almost complete ignorance of library needs and problems, resulting
inevitably in missed opportunities, waste motion, and un-
realized expectations. If we are to be more effective in

the field of overseas library development there must be more total planning which recognizes the book and the library as integral parts of any educational project. I should like to recommend that the foundations and government agencies seek the advice of a professional librarian whenever educational projects are under consideration or in the initial stages of planning. It is typical at present to call in the librarian after the grant has already been made to recommend how best to use the designated funds for objectives already determined. If a professional judgment were brought to bear when the objectives are being defined, many operational problems could be avoided and a more direct attack could be made on the professional aspects of the task.

Because my topic is the American role in overseas library development I have emphasized the changes that we must make to increase the effectiveness of our contribution. Changes, however, will have to occur on the other side as well, and while most of these are beyond our control, we can insist on certain safeguards. Any program of American assistance depends upon mutual agreements, and I think that we have been too lax in the past in seeking assurances that there is a real interest and a real commitment on the part of the recipient nation. Where grants are conferred to make possible the start of a new service, there should be as firm assurance as possible that the host country can and will continue to maintain it once American aid comes to an end. Perhaps the external financing should cover a longer period, but in progressively smaller proportions to permit the host country gradually to assume its responsibilities. There should be longer follow-through and periodic checks, less to police the project than to permit continuing advice and assistance as needed and wanted. If the necessary personnel, or facilities, or continuing support cannot be guaranteed, or if certain essential conditions for success cannot be met, the program should be deferred until they can. Far too many of our overseas projects have started out with great and optimistic éclat, only to stop dead, almost literally on the day after the grant ceased. This does not really help the foreign country, and almost assuredly harms us abroad.

In other countries, as here, the real need may be to educate the top administrators who make the decisions rather than those at the middle level who merely carry them out. On the library scene we have concentrated pretty much on the librarians, providing study grants and observation tours, offering consultation and advice within the library, sending an expert to set up and organize the library itself. But it is the ministers of education, the chancellors of universities, and the directors of the budget who will determine in what direction libraries will go and how much support they will receive. Until *they* understand the function of the library as an educational institution, until *they* recognize that organized information is a national resource, until *they* accept librarianship as a profession essential to the nation's welfare, most of our effort will be wasted. The need, as I suggested earlier, is a real one, but little will be done to meet it until it is a *felt* need — and felt at the level where determining decisions are made. We may have to adjust our sights for a higher target.

As I come to the end of this long recital of difficulties, problems, challenges, and tasks, it may seem to you that it is all too formidable, that the obstacles are greater than the rewards. But I once learned an interesting lesson in semantics from an old India hand who pointed out that things look much brighter if, every time we are inclined to use the word "problem," we substitute for it the word "opportunity." It works — and it works because it is really true. The difficult tasks before us (and I use the term "us" to include our foreign partners in this exchange as well) *are* opportunities to make an important contribution to the welfare of men and the nations they constitute. Foreign relations are, after all, only human relations complicated by some geographical and some psychological distances. I think, with patience and understanding, we are equal to the challenge — and the opportunity — they present.